REAL ESTATE RICHES

A Comprehensive Guide to Successful Investing

By

Richard B. Monger

- **Conclusion**

Introduction

Welcome to "Real Estate Riches: A Comprehensive Guide to Successful Investing." In this book, we will go on a trip through the intriguing and possibly rewarding world of real estate investing. Whether you are a newbie hoping to join the market for the first time or an experienced investor looking to fine-tune your strategy, this comprehensive book is intended to empower you with the information and skills required to prosper in the real estate sector.

Chapter 1 provides the groundwork by helping you obtain a comprehensive grasp of the real estate industry. We will investigate the mechanics of supply and demand, assess market cycles and trends, and learn how to locate prospective places ripe for investment possibilities.

In Chapter 2, we will go into developing a strong investing plan. By establishing your financial objectives and knowing your risk tolerance, you may build a strategy that corresponds with your desires. We will study numerous investing options

And risk assessment methodologies, ensuring you are well-prepared for the road ahead.

Financing is an essential component of real estate investing, and Chapter 3 will walk you through the process. We will study numerous financing choices, assess various mortgage kinds, and even investigate inventive funding methods that might help you get the required funds for your enterprises.

Chapter 4 focuses on discovering successful investment properties. From efficient property search tactics to calculating possible returns, you will learn the necessary procedures to locate real estate prospects that correspond with your investing goals. We will also study options for purchasing distressed properties that contain the potential for large returns.

Conducting comprehensive due diligence is crucial in any real estate acquisition, and this issue takes the front stage in Chapter 5. We will take you through the process of analyzing property worth and condition, exploring legal and zoning concerns, and validating property ownership and titles. Armed

With this information, you can make educated judgments with confidence.

Negotiation is an art, and Chapter 6 will teach you the skills essential to thrive in deal-making. Master negotiating skills, learn how to bargain with sellers, brokers, and buyers successfully, and understand how to build transactions that benefit all parties involved.

In Chapter 7, we explore the relevance of real estate investment tax methods. You will obtain a thorough grasp of the tax consequences of your investments and examine different approaches to using tax deductions and credits to improve your profits. Additionally, we will study tax-efficient holding arrangements to secure your money.

Effective property management is key to sustaining a profitable real estate portfolio, and Chapter 8 is devoted to this critical subject. Learn how to identify reputable property managers, perform tenant screenings, and construct efficient lease agreements. Additionally, we will cover best practices for property care and upkeep to maintain long-term profitability.

The current real estate world is molded by technology and data analytics, and Chapter 9 will assist you in exploiting their potential. Discover the newest tools and technologies accessible to real estate investors, and discover how to leverage data analytics to make well-informed choices that offer you a competitive advantage.

Finally, Chapter 10 covers the exciting potential of increasing your real estate portfolio. We will address methods for portfolio development, the balance between diversity and concentration, and explore long-term wealth-building tactics and exit plans.

By the conclusion of this book, you will be armed with the knowledge and confidence to pursue real estate investments effectively. Whether you aim to earn passive income, accumulate enormous wealth, or establish a broad investment portfolio, "Real Estate Riches" will be your guiding light on this rewarding path. So, let's dig in and open the door to your p prosperous future in real estate investment.

Chapter 1
Understanding the Real Estate Market

Welcome to the fascinating world of real estate investment! In this chapter, we'll dig into the basic components of understanding the real estate market, giving you the foundation you need to make educated investing choices. Whether you are a seasoned investor trying to extend your portfolio or a beginner ready to take your first step into the world of real estate, getting a full awareness of the market dynamics is vital to your success.

Section 1: The Dynamics of Supply and Demand

In real estate, supply and demand are the primary dynamics that impact property pricing and investment possibilities. Understanding these dynamics is vital for identifying possible profitable markets and making smart investment decisions. We'll analyze the elements that influence supply, such as new development, property availability, and inventory levels. Likewise, we'll explore the elements that affect demand, including population growth, economic indicators, and demographic trends.

Additionally, we'll take a deeper look at the idea of scarcity and how it influences property prices. Areas with limited land supply and strong demand tend to experience considerable appreciation over time, making them attractive prospects for long-term investment.

Section 2: Market Cycles and Trends

Real estate markets are prone to cycles, typified by periods of expansion, stability, downturn, and recovery. Understanding these cycles might help you schedule your investments properly and profit on market swings. We'll cover the phases of a typical real estate market cycle and how to spot them. Furthermore, we'll explore techniques to limit risk during market downturns and optimize rewards during moments of expansion.

Staying updated with current market developments is equally vital in making wise investing selections. We'll discuss rising trends in real estate, such as the emergence of sustainable homes, mixed-use projects, and the influence of technology on the business. By being well-informed on trends, you

May position yourself ahead of the curve and capture lucrative investment possibilities.

Section 3: Identifying Promising Locations

Location is one of the most essential variables determining real estate prices. A property's closeness to key services, schools, transit hubs, and job areas may considerably affect its popularity and potential for gain. In this part, we'll explore how to undertake detailed location research and identify up-and-coming communities with strong development potential.

Moreover, we'll touch on the need of completing a macroeconomic study of the area or city where you plan to invest. Economic variables, such as GDP growth, job markets, and company development, have a key effect in defining the overall demand for real estate in a given location.

Understanding the local housing market and its specific characteristics is equally vital. We'll lead you through the process of acquiring market data, monitoring median house prices, rental rates, and absorption rates. Armed with this knowledge, you

May make well-informed investment choices customized to the specificities of each local market.

By the conclusion of this chapter, you'll have a firm knowledge of the real estate market's key principles and elements that determine property prices. Armed with this information, you'll be better positioned to discover prospective investment prospects and begin on your road to real estate riches. So, let's get started!

The Dynamics of Supply and Demand

Welcome to the fascinating world of real estate investment! In this chapter, we will dig into the intriguing realm of supply and demand in the real estate market. As a knowledgeable investor, grasping how these factors interact and influence the property environment is vital for making educated choices that might lead you to real estate riches.

Supply and demand are the basic drivers of the real estate market, just like any other industry. When the supply of available properties equals or surpasses the demand from buyers or renters, it is generally referred to as a buyer's market. In this case, potential

Buyers have the upper hand, since sellers may be more prepared to bargain on price and conditions to clinch a deal.

Conversely, when demand surpasses supply, it becomes a seller's market. In such scenarios, sellers retain the edge, since they may charge higher prices and perhaps get numerous bids on their houses. This strong demand may be caused by several causes, including as excellent economic circumstances, population expansion, and increasing investment interest.

The relationship between supply and demand is not static; it varies throughout time, generating varied market circumstances. As an investor, it's crucial to be aware of these swings and understand how they might affect your investing plan.

Understanding Supply in the Real Estate Market

Supply refers to the number of properties available for sale or rent in a specific market. Several variables impact the supply of real estate:

A. New Construction: The pace at which new properties are created and added to the market plays a vital role in setting supply levels. Rapid building in a location might lead to an overstock, perhaps leading values to drop.

B. Property Availability: The amount of existing properties that are offered for sale or rent also influences supply. Higher numbers of available properties often equate to increasing supply.

C. Inventory Levels: Inventory refers to the total quantity of unsold or empty properties in a market. High inventory levels might imply an overstock, while low inventory levels signal limited alternatives for buyers or renters.

Understanding Demand in the Real Estate Market

Demand, on the other hand, refers to the number of purchasers or renters seeking homes in a certain market. Various reasons generate demand:

A. Population Growth: As populations rise, the need for housing likewise grows. Cities and areas

Experiencing strong population expansion frequently have more demand for real estate.

B. Economic Indicators: Economic factors, such as employment growth, income levels, and consumer confidence, directly influence housing demand. A thriving economy with plentiful employment opportunities tends to create increased demand.

C. Demographic Trends: Changes in demography, such as the number of millennials entering the housing market or an elderly population, might impact the sorts of houses in demand.

The Role of Scarcity in Real Estate

Scarcity is a significant issue in real estate that impacts both supply and demand dynamics. Properties situated in places with limited usable land and restricted space for additional buildings tend to be rare. In turn, this scarcity may push up property prices over time, making such regions appealing for long-term investment.

Understanding scarcity might help you find places or localities with great appreciation potential.

Additionally, it may aid you in determining the risk involved with investing in a region where land and property availability is ample.

As a real estate investor, comprehending the dynamics of supply and demand will help you to:

Identify developing market trends and hotspots with great potential for development.
Gauge the relative strength of different real estate markets to prioritize your investment options.
Adjust your strategy and techniques dependent on whether you are working in a buyer's or seller's market.
Make more educated pricing and negotiating choices to maximize your profits.
Keep in mind that the real estate market is varied, with each region and property type having its own distinct supply and demand characteristics. By consistently learning about market conditions and trends, you will be well-equipped to navigate the real estate world confidently.

Now that we've investigated the interesting world of supply and demand, let's move on to the next section: "Market Cycles and Trends." Understanding

These cycles will offer you vital insights into the ever-changing nature of the real estate industry. So, let's continue on this adventure to learn the secrets to successful real estate investment!

Market Cycles and Trends

Hey there, smart real estate investors! In this chapter, we'll take a deep dive into the intriguing world of real estate market cycles and trends. Understanding these cycles and being up-to-date with the current trends will offer you a considerable edge in making well-timed and lucrative investment selections. So, let's analyze the fundamentals of market cycles and how to profit from developing trends in the real estate business.

The Phases of a Real Estate Market Cycle

Real estate markets, like other economic sectors, go through cycles of growth, stability, recession, and recovery. As investors, it's crucial to understand these periods to change your tactics properly and optimize profits. We'll break down each process for you:

Expansion: During the expansion phase, economic growth is solid, and real estate demand is high. Property values tend to climb, and investment options are available. This is an ideal moment for active investing techniques, such as property flipping or construction initiatives.

Stability: The stability phase reflects a time of balanced supply and demand. Property values continue to increase, although at a slower rate. It's a time to concentrate on dependable income flow assets, such as rental properties, and to be wary about speculative initiatives.

Contraction: In the contraction phase, the market faces a slowdown, and demand diminishes. Property values may stagnate or possibly decrease somewhat. This era might be hard for investors, but it also gives chances for bargain shopping and distressed property buying.

Recovery: The recovery phase signifies the shift from a market slump to growth. Demand starts to take up again, leading to a rise in home prices. Savvy investors may position themselves to gain from the market's return.

Strategies for Each Market Phase

Now that you understand the distinct market stages, let's investigate specialized methods for each phase:

Expansion: During this phase, it's vital to be proactive and take advantage of advantageous circumstances. Seek for assets with great appreciation potential, and consider leveraging your investments to optimize rewards. However, use care not to overextend yourself in case the market turns.

Stability: In a stable market, concentrate on developing a robust portfolio with regular rental revenue. Consider spreading your assets across multiple property kinds and locales to lessen risk. Additionally, consider strategies to optimize your current assets for greater cash flow.

Contraction: In a downturn, you aim to safeguard your assets and capitalize on distressed opportunities. Keep a careful eye on the market, as motivated sellers could be eager to negotiate good bargains. Cash reserves and a good financial plan are vital to surviving this time.

Recovery: As the market starts to recover, be ready to respond rapidly. Properties bought at cheap rates during the downturn era may now produce large gains. Consider long-term investments in sectors that show significant signals of development.

Embracing Emerging Trends

The real estate sector is always developing, and keeping ahead of new trends may be a game-changer for your investment success. Let's review some significant themes impacting the market:

Sustainable Properties: With increased environmental awareness, properties that promote sustainability and energy efficiency are gaining favor. Investing in eco-friendly features not only helps the world but also attracts eco-conscious renters and purchasers.

Mixed-Use complexes: Urban regions are experiencing a boom in mixed-use complexes that blend residential, commercial, and recreational spaces. These projects build lively communities and give intriguing investment possibilities.

Technology Integration: Embrace technology innovations in the real estate market, such as virtual property tours, digital property management systems, and smart home automation. Leveraging technology may boost your property's attractiveness and simplify management activities.

Co-living and Co-working Spaces: The advent of remote work has raised the demand for co-living and co-working spaces. Consider investing in buildings that cater to this expanding trend, providing flexible and community living and working opportunities.

By embracing these trends and altering your investing strategy appropriately, you can position yourself for long-term success in the ever-changing real estate environment.

Congratulations! You've now obtained vital insights into market cycles and trends in the real estate business. Remember, great investors consistently educate themselves and stay adaptive to market volatility. Armed with this information, you're ready to navigate the dynamic real estate market with confidence and steer your way to real estate riches! Happy investing!

Identifying Promising Locations

Hello, clever real estate investors! In this chapter, we'll go deep into the fascinating process of discovering probable sites for your real estate investments. Choosing the correct location is a vital step that may make all the difference in your investment success. Whether you're contemplating residential homes, business operations, or rental properties, a well-researched and strategically located site may provide large rewards and long-term development.

Proximity to Essential Amenities

When analyzing a possible site, consider its closeness to vital facilities that people value in their everyday lives. These amenities may include schools, healthcare facilities, food shops, recreational spaces, and public transit hubs. Properties placed close to these attractions tend to generate increased demand from prospective purchasers or renters, pushing increasing property prices and rental costs.

We'll study the notion of walkability and how it affects property appeal. Areas with a high walkability score, where inhabitants can quickly reach facilities on foot, generally see considerable demand from both renters and purchasers. We'll also explain how to investigate and locate communities with plans for future expansion and improvements in infrastructure since these regions might provide fantastic investment prospects.

Economic Indicators and Job Markets

A robust employment market is a primary driver of real estate demand. When work possibilities abound in a given location, people migrate there to seek employment, producing a boom in demand for housing. As a consequence, property prices tend to climb, making it an appealing market for investors.

In this part, we'll lead you through completing a detailed investigation of the local economy. Look for cities or areas with stable or rising economies, varied sectors, and strong signs of employment growth. Additionally, consider the presence of big businesses and corporate offices, since they might function as magnets for housing demand.

Demographic Trends and Population Growth

Demographic patterns have a major impact on real estate investment choices. Analyzing population growth trends might help you discover places where demand for housing is projected to expand continuously over time. Look for cities or areas with an increasing population, especially those with an inflow of young professionals and families.

Consider aspects such as migration trends, birth rates, and aging populations to provide insights into the future housing demands of the region. Cities with a constant stream of new inhabitants are likely to experience ongoing demand for housing, making them appealing investment opportunities.

Crime Rates and Safety

Safety is a primary issue for prospective homeowners and renters. Neighborhoods with low crime rates and a reputation for safety tend to garner greater attention from both purchasers and renters. Research crime statistics and safety reports for the places you're considering to determine their appropriateness for investment.

Keep in mind that safety issues may drastically affect property prices and rental demand. Properties in safe communities may fetch higher prices and offer greater returns on investment in the long term.

Market Trends and Development Projects

Stay updated about current market trends and development initiatives in the region. Look for indicators of urban redevelopment, revival, or large-scale infrastructure initiatives that might favorably affect property prices. Areas experiencing tremendous growth and investment frequently provide good prospects for investors.

Take notice of new commercial hubs, mixed-use complexes, or transit improvements like new subway lines or motorways. These developments may alter the appeal of neighboring homes and lead to greater demand for housing.

Analyzing Supply and Demand Balance

Strike a balance between supply and demand in the desired region. An oversupply of available properties in a certain location may suggest a

Weaker market and therefore lower rental rates or property prices. On the other side, a scarcity of available properties might imply strong demand, making it hard to identify acceptable investment options.

Research the absorption rate, which evaluates the pace at which available properties are being sold or leased in a specific market. A balanced absorption rate reflects a steady real estate market with robust demand.

Considering Local Regulations and Zoning

Be careful of local legislation and zoning limitations that may affect your investing intentions. Different places may have particular zoning restrictions that regulate how properties may be utilized or developed. Familiarize yourself with these restrictions to ensure your investment matches the local laws.

Gathering Local Market Data

To make educated judgments, obtain local market data from credible sources. Real estate research,

Population data, and local market studies may give useful insights into property valuations, rental rates, vacancy rates, and historical patterns. Additionally, consult with local real estate agents or property management firms acquainted with the region to obtain personal information about the market dynamics.

Evaluating Potential for Future Growth

A successful real estate investment is not only about the present market circumstances but also about foreseeing the possibility of future development. Consider the growth potential of the location and examine how it corresponds with your long-term investment ambitions. Research prospective infrastructure projects, commercial developments, and plans for urban growth to determine the potential for appreciation and increasing demand.

Diversification and Risk Management

Finally, diversity is crucial to controlling risk in real estate investment. Consider diversifying your assets across several geographies and property kinds to decrease the effect of localized market changes.

Diversification may help you establish a solid and resilient portfolio.

In conclusion, choosing prospective places involves rigorous study, a sharp eye for market trends, and a profound awareness of local dynamics. By combining these criteria into your investing plan, you'll be well on your way to obtaining real estate riches. So, roll up your sleeves, and let's explore the most prospective investment sites together!

Chapter 2

Building a Solid Investment Strategy

Congratulations! You've taken the first step towards becoming a successful real estate investor by delving into the fascinating world of property investing. As you begin on this path, it's crucial to build the framework for a strong investing plan that corresponds with your financial objectives and risk tolerance.

Defining Your Financial Goals: Before going into any investment, it's vital to identify what you expect to accomplish via real estate. Ask yourself some essential questions:

What is your major objective? Are you seeking consistent rental income, long-term appreciation, or a mix of both?
What is your investing horizon? Are you seeking short-term profits or expecting to keep properties for the long haul?
How many funds do you have available to invest? Understanding your budget can help determine your investing strategy.

Are you looking for financial independence, retirement security, or certain financial milestones? Being clear about your financial objectives helps drive your decision-making process throughout your real estate investing journey. Having precise goals can help you stay focused and avoid distractions.

Choosing the Right Investment Approach:
Real estate provides diverse investing techniques, each catering to individual tastes and risk tolerances. Some typical techniques include:

Rental Properties: Investing in rental properties entails acquiring houses or flats to lease them to renters. Rental income may offer a stable cash flow, and properties may grow over time, accumulating equity.

Fix-and-Flip: If you have a talent for repairs and like converting dilapidated houses into diamonds, fix-and-flip could be the appropriate method for you. Buying homes below market value, remodeling them, and selling at a profit may be profitable but takes careful strategy and execution.

Real Estate Investment Trusts (REITs): For a more hands-off approach, consider investing in REITs, which are businesses that own, operate, or finance

Income-generating real estate. REITs are listed on major stock exchanges and provide investors with a way to engage in real estate without direct property ownership.

Real Estate Partnerships: Joining forces with other investors may offer up access to bigger projects and diversify risk. Real estate partnerships may take the form of joint ventures or limited partnerships, where investors share resources and skills.

Risk Assessment and Mitigation: Every investment comes with a certain degree of risk, and real estate is no different. However, by knowing and controlling these risks, you can secure your assets and boost your chances of success. Here are some risk factors to consider:

Market Risk: Real estate markets may change owing to economic circumstances, interest rates, and local considerations. Conduct rigorous market research to discover stable and expanding regions with significant potential.

Financing Risk: If you're leveraging borrowed money, be mindful of the risks connected with interest rates, loan conditions, and prospective market downturns that might influence your capacity to make mortgage commitments.

Tenant and Vacancy Risk: For rental properties, vacancies, and difficult tenants may harm your cash flow. Implement comprehensive tenant screening methods and put aside cash for possible vacancies.

Regulatory and Legal Risks: Stay current on local rules and regulations connected to real estate investments to avoid legal problems.

To reduce hazards, diversity is generally advised. Instead of putting all your wealth in a single property, try distributing it among many homes or investment kinds.

Remember, creating a sound investing plan is a continuous effort. Regularly examine your objectives, adapt your strategy, and keep updated about the real estate market to make well-informed judgments. Seek counsel from seasoned experts, network with other investors, and be open to learning from both achievements and setbacks. With a defined plan and a dedication to ongoing development, you're well on your way to reaching real estate riches!

Defining Your Financial Goals

Welcome to the fascinating world of real estate investment! One of the first and most critical stages on your road toward generating wealth via property investing is determining your financial objectives. Setting precise and well-defined goals will act as your guiding compass throughout your trip, helping you make educated choices and remain focused on what matters to you.

Understanding You're Why:
Take time to focus on why you want to invest in real estate. Is it to ensure a better financial future for yourself and your family? Are you seeking a passive income stream to complement your present salary or attain financial freedom? By knowing your motivations, you'll discover a deeper sense of purpose, which will keep you motivated through hard times and encourage you to keep going ahead.

Short-term and Long-term objectives: Consider both your short-term and long-term financial objectives. Short-term objectives might include obtaining your first investment property within a particular period or remodeling and selling a home for a fast return.

Long-term objectives can comprise creating a portfolio of rental properties to provide continuous income flow or striving to attain a specific amount of net worth by a given age. Having a combination of short-term successes and long-term goals produces a balanced and feasible strategy.

Quantifying Your Objectives: It's crucial to make your financial objectives measurable and quantitative. For instance, if your purpose is to produce a monthly passive income of $5,000 during the next five years, you have a clear target to strive towards. Specific statistics and deadlines can help you measure your progress and determine if you are on the correct road.

Assessing Your Risk Tolerance: Understanding your risk tolerance is crucial in designing a good investing plan. Real estate, like any investment, involves inherent risks. Some tactics, such as fix-and-flip, may entail greater short-term risks but possibly bigger rewards. On the other side, rental properties provide more consistent, long-term revenue but need constant maintenance. Assess your comfort level with risk and find financial

Opportunities that correspond with your temperament.

include Your Circumstances: Your financial objectives should also include your circumstances, such as your present financial condition, outstanding debts, employment stability, and family obligations. Real estate investment may be flexible and adaptable, so you can modify your strategy to match your scenario.

Aligning Real Estate with Your Whole Financial Strategy: Real estate should complement your whole financial strategy, not stand in isolation. Consider how real estate investing fits into your overall financial portfolio and retirement plan. Diversification is key, so assess how property investments might operate in harmony with other assets like stocks, bonds, and retirement funds.

Periodic Assessments and Adjustments: As life unfolds and circumstances change, it's vital to routinely assess and alter your financial objectives. You may face alterations in goals, financial capacities, or changes in the real estate market. Be

Open to reassessing and modifying your objectives to keep connected with your desires.

obtaining Professional counsel: If you're confused about how to define your financial objectives or need assistance building a thorough strategy, consider obtaining counsel from financial experts, real estate specialists, or mentors with knowledge in the industry. Their views and expertise might be crucial in defining your financial path.

Remember, the process of determining your financial objectives is a personal one. Take the time to soul-search, analyze the figures, and imagine the future you wish for. A well-crafted set of financial objectives will act as a roadmap to lead you through the dynamic and lucrative world of real estate investment. So, imagine big, establish your aims, and begin on this wonderful trip with confidence!

Choosing the Right Investment Approach

Congratulations on taking the first step toward developing a profitable real estate portfolio! As you begin your adventure into the world of real estate investing, one of the most crucial choices you'll

Make is picking the correct investment technique. The real estate market provides a varied variety of options, each with its benefits and problems. Let's review several prominent investing techniques to assist you select the one that corresponds best with your objectives and interests.

Rental Properties: Investing in rental properties is a conventional and time-tested technique for real estate investing. With this method, you acquire residential or commercial properties intending to lease them out to renters. Here are some crucial aspects to consider:

a. Steady Income: Rental properties may offer a consistent monthly cash flow from rental payments, enabling you to generate passive income over time.

b. Property Appreciation: In addition to rental income, properties may grow in value over the long run, thereby boosting your total wealth.

c. Tenant Management: Managing renters and property upkeep is a crucial part of this approach. You may opt to handle it yourself or employ a property management firm to help you.

Fix-and-Flip: If you have a flare for remodeling and like the exhilaration of turning houses around for a profit, fix-and-flip could be the plan for you. Here's what you should bear in mind:

a. Quick Returns: Fix-and-flip ventures attempt to acquire properties below market value, improve them, and sell them at a better price. This method may produce relatively rapid profits compared to long-term leases.

b. Renovation Expertise: Successful fix-and-flip investors have a sharp eye for finding homes with promise and know-how to conduct cost-effective repairs.

b. Market Timing: Market circumstances and property prices play a crucial part in this technique. Pay attention to market trends and estimate the demand for refurbished buildings in your selected region.

Real Estate Investment Trusts (REITs): If you want a more passive approach to real estate investment, consider investing in Real Estate Investment Trusts (REITs). These are firms that own, operate or

Finance income-generating real estate, and they sell shares to investors via the stock market. Here's why REITs could be appealing:

a. diversity: REITs frequently own a portfolio of assets across several industries and regions, offering rapid diversity for investors.

b. Liquidity: Unlike actual assets, REIT shares may be readily purchased or traded on major stock markets, enabling liquidity and flexibility.

c. Professional Management: REITs are managed by qualified experts, freeing investors of day-to-day property management tasks.

Real Estate Partnerships: Collaborating with other investors via real estate partnerships may be a great method to access bigger projects and share experience and resources. Here's what you should know about this approach:

a. Combined Resources: Real estate partnerships enable you to pool assets and share the financial burden of investments, allowing you to embark on more significant and possibly profitable projects.

B. Diversified talents: Partnering with people that bring varied talents and knowledge to the table will boost your chances of success and give you a well-rounded team.

c. Legal Agreements: When going into partnerships, it's vital to have clear legal agreements describing each party's obligations, profit-sharing arrangements, and exit alternatives.

When picking the correct investing technique, consider your risk tolerance, time commitment, and long-term financial objectives. Some investors may choose a combination of techniques to diversify their portfolio and decrease risk. Remember that no one strategy is better than another; it's about discovering what fits you best.

Research and education are crucial parts of making educated judgments. Attend real estate seminars, read books, join online forums, and network with experienced investors to get vital insights and expertise. Additionally, getting help from a real estate mentor or financial adviser may give vital support as you negotiate the complexity of real estate investment.

Keep in mind that real estate investing is a dynamic and ever-evolving sector. Be open to altering your plan as you acquire experience and as market circumstances change. With patience, determination, and a well-thought-out investing technique, you are on your way to establishing a real estate portfolio that may pave the route to financial independence and long-term riches. Happy investing!

Risk Assessment and Mitigation

Real estate investing may be a very lucrative enterprise, but it's not without its share of hazards. As you construct your investing plan, it's necessary to take a thorough approach to identify and manage possible risks. By doing so, you can secure your assets, boost your chances of success, and manage problems with confidence.

Market Risk: Market risk is an inherent aspect of every investment, and real estate is no different. Market circumstances may change owing to economic reasons, interest rates, supply and demand dynamics, and local developments. To analyze market risk effectively:

Conduct detailed market research: Analyze historical patterns, present circumstances, and future estimates for the region you're interested in. Look for economic statistics, employment growth, demographic trends, and big infrastructure projects that might impact the real estate market.

Diversify across markets: Investing in numerous geographic places might decrease your exposure to the ups and downs of a single market. Diverse markets might create a more stable overall portfolio.

Financing Risk: Using leverage to fund your real estate ventures may enhance rewards, but it also raises financing risk. Potential mitigations include:

Stress-test your finances: Before taking out a mortgage, examine your capacity to tolerate increased interest rates or times of lower income. Ensure you have adequate reserves to weather future financial crises.

Opt for fixed-rate mortgages: Fixed-rate mortgages give certainty, insulating you from interest rate changes. This may be particularly useful in a rising interest rate situation.

Tenant and Vacancy Risk: For rental property owners, tenant turnover and vacancies may

Dramatically impair cash flow. To reduce tenant and vacancy risks:

Thorough tenant screening: Implement a comprehensive tenant screening procedure to discover reputable and responsible tenants. Check credit records, rental references, and job history to estimate their capacity to satisfy rent responsibilities.

Tenant retention strategies: Foster strong landlord-tenant connections and handle tenant issues swiftly to support long-term tenancy.

Regulatory and Legal Risks: Real estate investments are subject to numerous rules and legal restrictions. Stay educated on local rules and ordinances that apply to property ownership and operation. Mitigations include:

Consult legal experts: Seek guidance from competent real estate lawyers to ensure you comply with all relevant rules and regulations.

Proper insurance coverage: Obtain comprehensive insurance plans to safeguard your investment from possible liabilities, natural catastrophes, and unanticipated incidents.

Property Condition and Maintenance Risks: Owning properties comes with the obligation of maintaining them to protect their value and attract renters or purchasers. To reduce property condition and maintenance risks:

Regular inspections: Conduct regular inspections to detect and solve maintenance concerns proactively. Prompt fixes may prevent small issues from growing into costlier ones.

Budget for maintenance: Set aside a percentage of rental revenue or cash flow for property upkeep and unanticipated repairs.

Economic Downturns: Economic downturns may affect property prices and rental demand. While it's impossible to foresee market cycles with accuracy, you may take efforts to prepare for economic downturns:

Cash reserves: Maintain adequate cash reserves to satisfy mortgage payments, property bills, and other financial commitments during hard economic conditions.

cautious underwriting: Avoid excessively optimistic assumptions in your investment calculations and use cautious growth estimates.

Remember, risk assessment and mitigation are continual activities. Regularly assess and adapt your risk management techniques as market circumstances and your portfolio develops. Engage with other experienced investors to learn from their risk management strategies and remain current on industry developments. By being proactive and vigilant in managing risks, you may create the framework for a resilient and successful real estate investing journey. Happy investing!

Chapter 3
Financing Your Real Estate Investments

Congratulations! You've chosen to enter into the exciting world of real estate investing. One of the critical aspects of successful real estate investment is knowing how to finance your projects effectively. In this chapter, we'll delve into various financing choices, review mortgage types, and explore creative funding solutions to help you make informed financial decisions and set a solid basis for your real estate journey.

Exploring Various Financing Options: a. Traditional Bank Loans: One of the most popular ways to finance real estate investments is through standard bank loans. These loans come with fixed or variable interest rates, and the amount you can borrow usually varies on your credit score, income, and the property's value. Before approaching a bank, it's important to ensure your credit score is in good shape and have a clear idea of your financial capabilities.

B. Private Lenders: Private lenders, also known as hard money lenders, are people or companies that provide short-term loans with higher interest rates and shorter payback terms. They are more flexible than traditional banks and can be a great choice if you need quick financing or have trouble getting a bank loan due to credit problems.

c. Real Estate Crowdfunding: In recent years, real estate crowdfunding sites have gained popularity as an alternative financing choice. These sites allow multiple investors to pool their funds together to invest in bigger projects. It's a fantastic way to diversify your investments and get involved in bigger real estate projects that might be beyond your financial capacity.

Evaluating Mortgage Types:
a. Fixed-Rate Mortgages: With a fixed-rate mortgage, your interest rate stays the same throughout the loan term, giving stability in your monthly payments. This choice is ideal for owners who prefer fixed costs and plan to hold onto the property for an extended time.

B. Adjustable-Rate Mortgages (ARMs): Unlike fixed-rate mortgages, ARMs have an interest rate that changes periodically based on market conditions. This can result in lower starting rates, but it also brings the possibility for higher payments if interest rates rise. ARMs are good for owners who plan to sell or refinance the property before the rate adjustment period starts.

c. Interest-Only Mortgages: Interest-only mortgages allow you to pay only the interest for a specific time, usually the first few years of the loan. After the initial time, you'll need to start paying capital as well. This choice can be advantageous for investors looking to increase cash flow during the early stages of ownership.

Creative Funding Solutions: a. Seller Financing: In some cases, the property seller may be ready to provide financing for the buy. This plan can offer benefits such as more flexible terms and possibly bypassing standard loan requirements. Negotiating selling credit terms can be a win-win situation for both parties involved.

B. Joint Ventures and Partnerships: Collaborating with other people through joint ventures or partnerships can help you handle more important projects and spread the financial load. It's crucial to create clear deals and describe each party's roles and tasks to ensure a successful relationship.

c. 1031 Exchange: If you already own an investment property and are looking to put in a new one, a 1031 exchange can help you avoid capital gains taxes. This powerful tool allows you to sell your current property and reinvest the proceeds into a like-kind property, offering possible tax benefits and preserving more capital for your next purchase.

In conclusion, financing your real estate investments requires careful thought and a full understanding of the available choices. Assess your financial position, study different financing methods, and don't be afraid to explore creative funding solutions to maximize your business potential. Remember, well-managed finance is the backbone of a successful real estate investment strategy, so take your time, seek professional help if needed, and start on your journey to build a lucrative real estate business.

Financing Your Real Estate Investments

Congratulations on taking the first steps toward building your real estate business! As you dive into the world of real estate investing, knowing the various financing choices available to you is crucial. In this chapter, we'll explore the ins and outs of different financial options to help you make informed choices and pave the way for a successful real estate business journey.

Traditional Bank Loans: Traditional bank loans are a tried-and-true way of financing real estate purchases. These loans are offered by banks and other financial institutions and come with set or changeable interest rates. The amount you can borrow will depend on factors such as your credit score, income, and the value of the property you plan to buy.

Pros:

Favorable interest rates: Bank loans often come with lower interest rates compared to other financing choices, which can positively impact your cash flow and total profitability.

Longer repayment terms: Bank loans typically offer longer repayment times, making it more manageable to service the debt over time.

Established process: Since traditional bank loans are a popular financing method, the application process is well-defined, and you can expect a clear timeline for acceptance.

Cons:

Stringent requirements: Banks may have strict eligibility criteria, needing a high credit score and a sizeable down payment, which can be difficult for new investors.

Lengthy approval process: Obtaining a bank loan can take time due to extensive paperwork and review processes, which might not be ideal for time-sensitive deals.

Private Lenders (Hard Money Lenders): Private lenders, often referred to as hard money lenders, offer short-term loans that cater to buyers looking for quick financing or those facing challenges in getting traditional bank loans. Private lenders are more open and focus less on the borrower's credit score, putting greater stress on the property's value and potential.

Pros:

Quick access to funds: Private lenders can expedite the loan approval process, providing you with the necessary funds in a shorter timeframe, and allowing you to seize time-sensitive business chances.
Less focus on credit score: Hard money lenders consider the property's value and the investment's potential more than the borrower's credit past, making it feasible for owners with less-than-ideal credit scores.
Cons:

Higher interest rates: Private lenders typically charge higher interest rates compared to traditional banks, which can impact your cash flow and total success.
Shorter repayment terms: Hard money loans often have shorter repayment periods, meaning you'll need to have an exit plan in place to either sell the property or refinance within the stated timeframe.

Real Estate Crowdfunding: In recent years, real estate crowdfunding has emerged as a popular alternative financing choice, revolutionizing how

Investors join in bigger real estate projects. Crowdfunding sites bring together multiple buyers who pool their funds to invest in specific real estate options.

Pros:

Diversification: Real estate crowdfunding allows you to invest in a range of properties across different places and types, lowering risk and diversifying your investment portfolio.

Access to larger deals: Through crowdfunding, you can join in projects that would otherwise be beyond your financial capacity, giving you exposure to bigger and possibly more lucrative opportunities.

Cons:

Limited control: When spending through crowdfunding platforms, you may have limited control over the decision-making process, leaving key choices to the project's sponsor or boss.

Investment fees: Crowdfunding sites often charge fees for their services, which can affect your total returns. Be sure to carefully review the fee structure before agreeing to any investment.

Navigating the financial scene is an important part of your real estate business journey. As you evaluate different financing choices, consider your financial goals, risk tolerance, and investment strategy. Each financing method comes with its own set of advantages and disadvantages, so take the time to fully study and seek professional help when required. With a well-thought-out financing plan, you'll be better able to make confident business choices and set yourself up for a prosperous future in real estate. Happy buying!

Evaluating Mortgage Types

When it comes to financing your real estate investments, choosing the right mortgage type is a critical choice that can greatly impact your investment's success. Understanding the various mortgage options available and comparing their fit to your financial goals is important for making informed choices. In this part, we'll explore different mortgage types, their benefits, and their possible drawbacks to help you select the most suitable choice for your real estate endeavors.

Fixed-Rate Mortgages: Fixed-rate mortgages are one of the most common and popular kinds of mortgages among real estate owners. With a fixed-rate mortgage, the interest rate stays constant throughout the loan term, giving predictability and security in your monthly payments. This consistency allows you to plan your finances with security, as you'll know exactly how much you need to spend for the mortgage payment each month.

Advantages:

Predictable Payments: As mentioned earlier, fixed-rate mortgages offer consistent monthly payments, which can be particularly helpful when planning for your investment property.
Long-Term Planning: Investors who plan to hold onto their property for an extended time can benefit from knowing that their mortgage interest rate won't change, regardless of market changes.
Drawbacks:

Higher Initial Rates: Fixed-rate mortgages may have slightly higher interest rates compared to adjustable-rate mortgages (ARMs) during the initial years of the loan.

Potentially Higher Costs: If market interest rates drop greatly, you won't benefit from the lower rates unless you refinance, which could involve additional costs.

Adjustable-Rate Mortgages (ARMs): Adjustable-rate mortgages (ARMs) offer an option to fixed-rate mortgages. With an ARM, the interest rate is originally cheaper than a fixed-rate mortgage but adjusts periodically based on market conditions. The adjustment times can vary, but common stages include one, three, five, or seven years.

Advantages:

Lower Initial Rates: ARMs typically come with lower initial interest rates, making them an attractive choice for investors who expect interest rates to stay stable or drop in the short term.

Flexibility: If you plan to sell or refinance the property before the rate adjustment time, an ARM can offer flexibility and possible cost savings.

Drawbacks:

Rate Uncertainty: The main drawback of ARMs is the uncertainty linked with future rate changes. If

Interest rates rise greatly, your mortgage payments could increase, possibly impacting your cash flow.

Market Volatility: ARMs are more susceptible to changes in the market, which can make financial planning more difficult.

Interest-Only Mortgages: Interest-only mortgages allow investors to make lower monthly payments during the initial time of the loan, usually running from five to ten years. During this time, you only pay the interest part of the mortgage, and the principal stays fixed.

Advantages:

Enhanced Cash Flow: By paying only the interest, your monthly payments are greatly reduced, allowing you to maximize your cash flow during the interest-only time.

Investment Leverage: Interest-only mortgages can provide owners with greater leverage, allowing them to shift their capital to other investments or projects.

Drawbacks:

Balloon Payments: At the end of the interest-only time, you'll be expected to start paying both the

Interest and the principal, resulting in higher monthly payments.

Equity Building: Since you're not paying down the debt during the interest-only time, your equity in the property will not grow unless property prices advance.

In conclusion, analyzing mortgage types is a crucial step in financing your real estate purchases. Consider your short-term and long-term financial goals, risk tolerance, and market conditions when deciding between fixed-rate mortgages, adjustable-rate mortgages (ARMs), and interest-only mortgages. Each mortgage type has its benefits and drawbacks, and there is no one-size-fits-all answer. Work closely with a trusted mortgage advisor or financial professional to understand your options fully and make a well-informed choice that fits with your investment strategy. Remember, the right mortgage choice can play a key role in helping you achieve real estate business success.

Creative Funding Solutions

When it comes to financing your real estate investments, thinking outside the box can lead to unique and innovative solutions. In this section, we'll explore creative funding options that can help you overcome financial barriers, seize opportunities, and expand your real estate portfolio.

Seller Financing:
Seller financing, also known as owner financing or seller carryback, is a creative funding solution where the property seller acts as the lender. Instead of seeking a traditional bank loan, the buyer negotiates with the seller to make payments directly to them over an agreed-upon period. This approach can be beneficial for both parties involved:

For Buyers:

Easier qualification: Seller financing may be more accessible than bank loans, especially if the buyer has less-than-perfect credit or limited financial history.

Flexible terms: Buyers can negotiate more flexible repayment terms, interest rates, and down payment requirements with the seller.

Lower closing costs: Traditional closing costs associated with bank loans may be reduced or eliminated in seller financing deals.

For Sellers:

Attracting buyers: Offering seller financing can make the property more attractive to potential buyers, especially in a competitive market or when selling unique properties.

Steady income stream: Sellers can enjoy a steady stream of income from the monthly payments received from the buyer.

Faster sale: Seller financing can expedite the selling process, as buyers may be more inclined to purchase when traditional financing options are limited.

Joint Ventures and Partnerships:

Forming a joint venture or partnership with other investors can open up new avenues for funding larger real estate projects. In a joint venture, two or more parties pool their resources, skills, and expertise to invest in a particular property or development. Partnerships can be structured in various ways, such as:

Equity Partnerships: Each partner contributes funds to purchase and operate the property, and profits are distributed based on the percentage of ownership.

Silent Partnerships: One partner provides the funding while the other manages the property and operations.

General and Limited Partnerships: General partners manage the investment and are responsible for decision-making, while limited partners contribute funds but have limited involvement in management decisions.

Joint ventures and partnerships offer several benefits, including:

Shared risk: The financial burden is divided among partners, reducing individual exposure to risk.

Access to expertise: Partnering with experienced investors brings valuable knowledge and skills to the table.

Access to larger projects: Pooling resources allows investors to participate in more substantial deals that would be challenging to undertake individually.

Real Estate Crowdfunding:

Real estate crowdfunding platforms have revolutionized the way investors can participate in larger real estate projects. Through crowdfunding,

Multiple investors pool their funds online to invest in a specific property or real estate development. Crowdfunding offers several advantages:

Diversification: Investors can spread their funds across multiple projects, reducing the risk associated with investing in a single property.

Access to prime opportunities: Crowdfunding platforms often feature projects curated by experienced real estate professionals, providing access to high-quality investments.

Lower capital requirements: Crowdfunding allows investors to participate in projects with lower minimum investment amounts compared to traditional real estate investments.

Creative Financing Techniques:

a. Lease Options: Lease options, also known as rent-to-own agreements, allow the buyer to lease the property with the option to purchase it at a predetermined price and within a specified time frame. This arrangement provides time for the buyer to build up their credit or save for a down payment while occupying the property.

b. Hard Money Loans: Hard money loans are short-term, asset-based loans that are secured by the

Property itself. These loans are often provided by private lenders or investor groups and are ideal for quick purchases or property renovations.

c. Self-Directed IRAs: If you have a self-directed Individual Retirement Account (IRA), you can invest in real estate directly, allowing your retirement funds to grow through property appreciation and rental income.

d. House Hacking: House hacking involves living in one unit of multifamily property and renting out the other units. This creative strategy can help offset your living expenses while building equity in the property.

In conclusion, creative funding solutions can open up a world of possibilities for real estate investors. Whether it's through seller financing, joint ventures, crowdfunding, or creative financing techniques, exploring these innovative options can help you overcome financial hurdles and accelerate your path to building a successful real estate portfolio. As you embark on your investment journey, always seek professional advice when needed and stay open to

Unconventional approaches that align with your financial goals and risk tolerance. Happy investing!

Chapter 4
Finding Profitable Investment Properties

Congratulations! You've now got a strong knowledge of the real estate market, improved your business strategy, and secured capital for your projects. The next crucial step in building your real estate riches is to find profitable investment homes. This chapter will guide you through various techniques and important tips to help you spot those gems that will fuel your success.

The Power of Study: Before you start on your property search journey, take the time to do a thorough study. Investigate the local real estate market, economic situations, and growth trends in the places you're interested in. Study population growth, job prospects, infrastructure development, and features that draw tenants or buyers. Look into past property data and price trends to spot possible chances and avoid overpriced areas.

Define Your Investment Criteria: One size does not fit all in real estate investment. Different investors have different tastes and risk appetites. Clearly

Describe your financial requirements to narrow down your search. Determine the property type, such as single-family houses, multi-unit properties, business buildings, or vacant land. Decide on the site, size, price, and expected returns on investment. This clarity will make it easier to sort through the vast array of available features.

Networking and Relationships: Real estate is not just about numbers; it's also about people. Establishing a strong network in the industry can open doors to secret opportunities. Attend area real estate networking events, join investment clubs, and participate in internet groups. Engage with real estate agents, traders, property owners, and other investors. Building meaningful connections will not only help you find properties but also provide useful insights and tips.

Work with Real Estate Agents: Experienced real estate agents can be useful tools in your property search. They have access to a wide range of offerings, including off-market and pocket listings that might not be open to the public. A skilled agent who knows your investment goals can help you find suitable properties quickly. Communicate your goals

Clearly, and stay involved with your agent throughout the process.

Online Listing Platforms and Tools: The internet has changed the way real estate is bought and sold. Utilize online listing tools and real estate markets to browse properties that fit your standards. Websites like Zillow, Realtor.com, and LoopNet can be excellent tools. Moreover, consider using property search tools that offer filters to cut down your choices based on price, area, property type, and other factors.

Drive and Walk Around: Don't underestimate the power of personally visiting neighborhoods and properties. Take a drive or a walk around the places you're interested in. This will give you a sense of the neighborhood's atmosphere, services, and possibility for future growth. Keep an eye out for "For Sale" signs and damaged homes that may not be listed online.

Direct Marketing and Letters: Consider applying direct marketing methods to reach property owners who may not have listed their properties but might be interested in selling. Send personalized messages

Expressing your interest in buying their home. A well-crafted letter can start conversations and lead to possible deals.

Real Estate Auctions: Auctions can be a great way to find investment homes at low prices. Many homes are sold through bids due to foreclosure, tax liens, or estate sales. Attend local sales or discover online sites that host real estate auctions. Be sure to study the properties carefully before bidding.

Wholesalers and Real Estate Wholesaling: Wholesalers are investors who find off-market properties and pass them on to other owners. Partnering with wholesalers can give you access to exclusive deals that fit your business standards. Network with suppliers and consider joining meetups or events where they might be present.

Creative Marketing: If you have a particular place or property type in mind, get creative with your marketing. Consider putting "I Buy Houses" signs in key areas, or create eye-catching flyers that market your interest in buying homes. This method can lead to direct requests from motivated sellers.

Remember, finding profitable investment homes is a skill that improves with practice. Stay persistent, be patient, and keep refining your plan as you learn from each chance. The more properties you evaluate and study, the better you'll become at finding those that will add to your real estate wealth. Happy hunting!

Chapter 5
Conducting Due Diligence

When it comes to dealing with real estate, due diligence is a critical step that should never be ignored. It includes fully studying and investigating a property before finalizing a buy. Conducting proper due research helps you make informed choices, avoid possible problems, and ensure that you are investing in a property that fits with your financial goals. In this chapter, we'll dig into the essential aspects of conducting due diligence, equipping you with the information and tools to confidently assess the viability of a real estate purchase.

Assessing Property Value and Health: Before getting into any real estate deal, it's important to determine the true value of the property and examine its health. Start by completing a comparative market analysis (CMA) to rate similar properties in the area that have recently sold. This will provide you with an idea of the property's market value. Engage the services of a skilled appraiser to receive a neutral professional opinion on the property's worth.

Inspecting the physical state of the property is equally important. Hire a qualified inspector to fully evaluate the construction, plumbing, electrical systems, roof, base, and general building integrity. Any possible problems or necessary repairs can greatly impact your investment's profitability. Be sure to request a thorough inspection report to help in your decision-making process.

Investigating Legal and Zoning Matters: The legal parts of a real estate purchase can be complicated and require careful attention. Verify the property's legal status by reviewing title deeds, encumbrances, liens, and any unpaid bills or taxes. A real estate attorney can be a valuable tool in helping you manage these legal difficulties and ensure a clean and usable title.

Inquire about planning laws and property usage limits. Understanding how the land can be used and whether there are any zoning limitations can influence your business plan. Ensure that the property's current use meets with local zoning laws and that there are no plans for big projects nearby that might negatively affect the property's value.

Confirming Property Ownership and Titles: One of the most critical parts of due diligence is confirming the property's ownership and titles. Ensure that the seller has the legal power to pass ownership and that there are no conflicts regarding ownership. Request a title search and title insurance to protect yourself from any unforeseen title flaws that could damage your investment in the future.

Analyzing rented and Lease Agreements (For Rental Properties): If you are considering an income-generating property, such as rented real estate, carefully review all current lease agreements. Analyze the terms of the leases, rental rates, security payments, and lease end dates. Understanding the present rental income and the tenant's payment history can provide insights into the property's cash flow possibilities.

Evaluating Financial Statements (For Commercial Properties): For commercial real estate purchases, request the property's financial statements, including income and spending reports. Analyze the property's past financial success to gauge its profitability. Assess the vacancy rate and lease terms of business

Buildings to determine the security of the renting income.

Environmental and Safety Concerns: Environmental issues can greatly impact a property's value and pose possible liability risks. Conduct an environmental review to find any past or present contamination issues. Additionally, consider the safety and security of the property's location, as these factors can affect both the property's worth and its appeal to possible tenants or buyers.

In conclusion, performing due research is a crucial step in the real estate investment process. Take the time to fully study and investigate the property to ensure that you make informed choices and protect your investment capital. Enlist the knowledge of real estate professionals, such as inspectors, evaluators, lawyers, and real estate managers, to help you through the due diligence process successfully. By being diligent in your investigations, you can maximize your chances of finding a lucrative real estate purchase that fits with your financial goals and brings you long-term success.

Chapter 6
Negotiation Strategies and Deal Making

Congratulations, smart investor! You've hit a crucial part in your journey toward Real Estate Riches. Negotiation skills are the backbone of successful real estate investments. In this chapter, we'll dive deep into the art of negotiating, providing you with the tools and strategies to secure the best deals possible.

The Power of Preparation: Before starting any deal, remember the age-old adage: "Failing to prepare is preparing to fail." Arm yourself with detailed study and information about the property, market conditions, and the seller's motivations. Understanding the seller's perspective and needs will allow you to build an appealing offer that meets their requirements while ensuring your financial goals are met.

Active Listening and Empathy: Effective bargaining is not about overpowering the other party; it's about finding common ground and building win-win situations. Practice active listening to understand the seller's worries, fears, and goals. Empathize with

Their position and show real interest in finding a mutually beneficial answer. Building friendship and trust can go a long way in creating a positive bargaining environment.

Establish Your Walk-Away Point: Know your financial limits and the terms that would make the business no longer possible for you. It's important to have a clear walk-away point and stick to it. Sometimes, the best deal is the one you didn't make. Avoid getting personally connected to a home, as it may lead to compromising on crucial aspects that could affect your returns.

Start with Your Best Offer: In certain scenarios, giving your best offer right from the start can signal your seriousness and willingness to make a fair deal. It also helps in establishing the discussion around your desired terms. However, be careful not to overextend yourself, and always leave room for some discussion.

Use Objective Criteria: Base your talks on objective criteria rather than feelings. Rely on market info, similar property prices, and the property's condition to back your offer. This method helps both sides

Move away from subjective feelings and focus on the facts, making it easier to reach an agreement.

Creative Solutions: Real estate talks are not always limited to the price. Be open to exploring creative options that help both you and the seller. For instance, you could offer a faster closing date, take certain duties (e.g., fixes), or create a seller finance arrangement. Such choices can sweeten the deal for the seller and provide you with good terms.

Handling Counteroffers: Receiving a counteroffer is normal during talks. Take your time to assess it carefully. If the terms are close to what you're looking for, consider making a counter-counteroffer that covers the remaining gap. Keep the lines of dialogue open and be respectful throughout the process.

Know When to Bring in Professionals: In some cases, negotiations can become complicated or highly charged. Knowing when to bring in a professional real estate agent or a skilled mediator can be useful. Their knowledge and impartial viewpoint can help enable smoother talks and bridge gaps between parties.

Document Everything: Once an agreement is made, ensure that all discussed terms are properly written in the contract. Review the deal carefully and seek legal help if necessary to avoid possible problems.

Maintain connections: Real estate is a small world, and having good connections with buyers, agents, and other owners can lead to future possibilities. Even if talks don't end in a deal, treating everyone with respect and professionalism can leave a lasting impression.

Negotiation skills take time and practice to learn, but they are important to your success in real estate investing. Be patient, determined, and always keep your long-term goals in mind. With the right method, you'll become a master negotiator and open even more chances for Real Estate Riches!

Chapter 7
Real Estate Investment Tax Strategies

Welcome to Chapter 7 of "Real Estate Riches: A Comprehensive Guide to Successful Investing!" In this chapter, we will explore the often complicated and critical part of the real estate business - tax tactics. Understanding and improving your tax position can significantly impact your investment returns, so we'll take a friendly and helpful approach to help you understand this important area.

The Importance of Tax Planning

Tax planning is an important part of successful real estate buying. It includes structuring your investments in a way that minimizes tax debt and improves after-tax profits. When you own real estate, you may face various tax consequences, including property taxes, income taxes, capital gains taxes, and more. By taking a proactive approach to tax planning, you can keep more of your hard-earned money and ensure your investments are as tax-efficient as possible.

Understanding Real Estate Taxation

Before getting into specific methods, it's important to have a strong grasp of how real estate is taxed. Different types of real estate purchases, such as rental properties, fix-and-flips, and business properties, are subject to different tax rules. Additionally, your tax responsibilities may vary based on your position as an individual owner, a real estate partnership, or a business.

We'll study topics like depreciation, which allows you to deduct a part of the property's value each year, and capital gains tax, which is applicable when you sell an investment property at a profit. Moreover, we'll discuss the impact of passive income rules and how they affect real estate buyers.

Utilizing Tax Deductions and Credits

One of the most effective ways to lower your taxable income is to take advantage of tax deductions and credits available to real estate owners. These tax breaks can include costs linked to property upkeep, repairs, property management fees, and mortgage interest. Properly documenting and organizing your spending can make a big difference in the amount of taxes you owe.

We'll provide you with a thorough list of possible deductions and credits, ensuring you don't miss out on valuable tax-saving chances. However, it's crucial to remain legal with tax laws, so we'll also discuss the value of record-keeping and working with qualified tax experts.

Tax-Efficient Holding Structures

Choosing the right holding structure for your real estate purchases can greatly impact your total tax bill and protect your assets. We'll discuss the benefits and downsides of different holding structures, such as having properties individually, making limited liability companies (LLCs), or utilizing real estate investment trusts (REITs).

Moreover, we'll study the benefits of 1031 exchanges, which allow you to defer capital gains taxes by reinvesting the funds from the sale of one property into another like-kind property. Properly performed, 1031 exchanges can be a powerful tool for building your real estate business while deferring tax payments.

Tax Planning for Long-Term Wealth Building

As you grow in your real estate investment journey, your tax strategy may change along with your financial goals. We'll cover long-term tax planning considerations, including estate planning and succession methods, ensuring your wealth is efficiently passed to your heirs.

Furthermore, we'll talk about how to match your tax approach with your investment exit plan. Whether you plan to keep properties for the long term or engage in strategic portfolio diversification, having a well-thought-out exit strategy can help you reduce possible tax consequences when selling your properties.

Conclusion:

Understanding and adopting effective tax strategies are crucial for any real estate owner looking to build lasting wealth and maximize returns. By optimizing your tax situation, you can keep more of your income, reinvest efficiently, and grow your real estate business successfully.

Remember, tax laws can change over time, so it's important to stay informed and work with

Experienced tax advisors who specialize in real estate investments. With the right understanding and method, you'll be well on your way to achieving real estate riches through smart tax planning!

Chapter 8
Property Management and Maintenance - Ensuring Your Investments Thrive

Congratulations! You've successfully bought a real estate business property. Now comes the crucial part of ensuring your investment grows and provides you with steady returns: effective property management and care. This chapter will guide you through the essential aspects of handling your properties like a pro, keeping renters happy, and maintaining the long-term value of your investments.

Section 1: The Role of Property Management
Property management is the backbone of a successful real estate business. It includes overseeing the day-to-day operations of your properties and ensuring they stay profitable and well-maintained. Whether you decide to handle your properties personally or hire a professional property management company, knowing the key duties is vital.

1.1 Tenant Relations and Screening

A key duty of property management is finding and keeping quality tenants. Learn how to perform thorough tenant screenings, including background checks, credit history reviews, and previous rental references. Building good tenant relations will support longer leases and lower vacancy rates, helping your bottom line.

1.2 Lease Agreements and Legal Compliance
Explore the parts of a well-structured lease deal that protects both your interests and those of your renters. Understand local landlord-tenant rules and regulations to ensure you stay current, avoiding costly legal issues in the process.

1.3 Rent Collection and Financial Management
Efficient rent gathering is important to keeping consistent cash flow. Discover strategies to simplify the rent collection process and how to handle late payments properly. Additionally, learn how to handle property-related funds successfully, including budgeting for costs and handling security deposits.

Section 2: Property Maintenance and Upkeep

Keeping your rental homes in excellent shape is important for attracting and keeping renters while Protecting the property's value over time. Learn how to build a proactive maintenance plan and handle different maintenance jobs.

2.1 Regular Property Inspections

Performing regular property inspections helps spot upkeep needs early on, stopping possible issues from escalating. We'll cover best practices for performing checks and making inspection checklists.

2.2 Handling Repairs and Emergencies

From minor repairs to unexpected situations, being prepared is vital. Understand how to organize and share repair tasks efficiently, and build relationships with reliable workers to ensure prompt and cost-effective solutions.

2.3 Preventative Maintenance Strategies

Discover the value of preventative maintenance in reducing total repair costs and improving tenant happiness. Implement preventative repair plans for different property components, such as HVAC systems, plumbing, and roofs.

Section 3: Technology and Property Management
Embrace technology to reduce property management chores and improve efficiency.

3.1 Property Management Software
Explore the various property management tools available, which can automate chores such as rent collection, lease management, and tenant contact, eventually saving you time and effort.

3.2 Smart Home Technology
Learn about adding smart home technology to your properties to attract modern renters, increase property value, and improve the energy economy.

Section 4: Scaling Your Property Management Business
As your real estate portfolio grows, you might consider expanding your property managing services or outsourcing them to pros. This part will cover both options.

4.1 In-House vs. Third-Party Property Management
Understand the benefits and drawbacks of handling properties in-house versus getting a third-party

property management business. Consider things like cost, control, and time investment.

4.2 Building a Property Management Team

If you decide to handle properties in-house, learn how to build and lead a skilled property management team, ensuring efficient operations and excellent tenant relations.

In conclusion, effective property management and care are the keys to the long-term success of your real estate assets. By prioritizing tenant happiness, implementing proactive repair practices, and utilizing technology, you can build a thriving collection of properties that will give consistent returns and grow your wealth over time.

Chapter 9
Leveraging Technology and Data Analytics

In today's fast-paced and interconnected world, technology and data analytics have become necessary tools for successful real estate owners. The ability to harness these tools can provide invaluable insights, streamline processes, and eventually lead to more informed choices. In this chapter, we'll explore the various ways you can utilize technology and data analytics to maximize your real estate business efforts.

Harnessing Real Estate Technology: The real estate business has seen a rise in technological developments in recent years. From online property sites to virtual tours, these innovations have revolutionized the way properties are bought, sold, and handled. As an investor, it's important to familiarize yourself with these tools to gain a competitive edge. Some key areas of real estate technology include:

Online Listing Platforms: Websites and apps that aggregate property listings from various sources, making it easier to discover possible business possibilities.

Virtual Reality (VR) and Augmented Reality (AR): Cutting-edge technologies that allow investors to tour homes afar, saving time and money in the process.

Real Estate Crowdfunding: Platforms that allow investors to pool their funds and invest in bigger real estate projects collectively.

Using Data to Make Informed Decisions: Data analytics is a powerful tool that allows real estate investors to study trends, measure market conditions, and find good investment chances. Here's how you can use info effectively:

Market Research: Accessing market data such as property prices, rental rates, and vacancy rates can help you gauge the health of a particular market and find places with growth potential.

Comparable Sales Analysis: Analyzing recent sales of similar properties in the target area can provide insights into property prices and possible profits.

Rental Market Analysis: Understanding rental demand and average rental rates in a specific area Can help you determine the possible rental income of an investment property.

Demographic and Economic Trends: Studying demographic and economic data can show the general attractiveness and sustainability of a market.

Real Estate Investment Software and Tools: Investing in real estate involves organizing vast amounts of information and handling multiple processes simultaneously. Thankfully, there are numerous software solutions and tools meant to simplify and improve real estate investing activities. Some popular types of real estate investment tools include:

Property Management Software: These tools help streamline chores related to property management, such as rent collection, renter screening, repair tracking, and financial reporting.

Financial Analysis Software: These tools help in evaluating possible business sites, calculating returns on investment, and performing cash flow analysis.

Customer Relationship Management (CRM) Software: CRMs help investors and agents handle leads, track contacts, and improve customer relationships.

Project Management Software: If you're interested in real estate development or renovation projects, project management software can help you plan tasks, timelines, and budgets successfully.

Embracing Smart Home Technology: As the Internet of Things (IoT) continues to grow, smart home technology is becoming increasingly popular in the real estate market. Investors can capitalize on this trend by adding smart gadgets and automation systems to their rental homes. Smart home features such as automated lighting, temperature control, security systems, and smart locks can improve the property's appeal, increase tenant happiness, and even lower running costs.

By embracing technology and data analytics in your real estate investing journey, you can gain a competitive edge, make more informed choices, and position yourself for long-term success. Remember to stay updated on the latest advancements in real estate technology, and don't hesitate to adopt new Tools that match your business goals. Embracing technology will not only streamline your processes but also improve the general experience for both you and your renters.

Harnessing Real Estate Technology

In today's fast-paced and ever-evolving real estate environment, technology has emerged as a game-changer for buyers. From online property sites to virtual tours and smart home technology, these innovations have revolutionized the way properties are bought, sold, and controlled. In this chapter, we'll dig deeper into the world of real estate technology and explore how you can effectively harness its potential to boost your investment strategies and stay ahead in the competitive market.

Online Property Listing Platforms: The rise of online property listing platforms has changed the way properties are displayed and found. These platforms aggregate property offerings from various sources, including real estate companies, property developers, and individual sellers, making it easy for investors to explore a wide range of choices from the comfort of their homes. Friendly user interfaces And advanced search tools help you narrow down your choices based on area, price range, property type, and more. By employing these platforms, you can easily spot possible business chances and gain valuable insights into market trends.

Virtual Reality (VR) and Augmented Reality (AR) Technologies:
Virtual Reality and Augmented Reality are cutting-edge technologies that have changed the property-watching experience. VR allows buyers to take virtual tours of properties afar, giving a lifelike and immersive experience as if they were physically present at the site. AR, on the other hand, overlays digital information in the real world, allowing investors to view additional property data and possible modifications. These technologies save important time and resources, especially when considering homes located in faraway or international markets. Embracing VR and AR can help you make well-informed decisions without the need for extensive travel.

Real Estate Crowdfunding Platforms: Crowdfunding has gained significant popularity in the real estate industry, offering an innovative way for investors to Pool their funds and join in bigger real estate projects that would have been otherwise out of reach. Real estate crowdfunding sites connect investors with property developers or sponsors looking to raise cash for their projects. As an investor, you can diversify your business portfolio by adding to various projects across different property types and regions. Additionally, crowdfunding provides a chance for passive investment, where you can let experienced experts handle the property management aspects.

Property Management Software: Effective property management is important for keeping the worth and revenue of your rental properties. Property management software offers a complete answer for landlords and property managers to streamline various tasks, from rent collection and lease management to repair tracking and financial reporting. These platforms often feature tenant portals that allow renters to send repair requests and make online rental payments, improving their overall experience. By adopting property management software, you can improve productivity, reduce administrative burdens, and increase contact with renters.

Financial Analysis Tools: Investing in real estate needs careful financial analysis to assess the possible profitability of a property. Financial analysis tools, often offered as web-based applications or mobile apps, help you evaluate various parts of an investment, including cash flow projections, return on investment (ROI), and capitalization rates. These tools take into account things like property purchase price, financing terms, rental income, running costs, and market conditions. By using financial analysis tools, you can make data-driven choices and find high-yield investment possibilities.

Customer Relationship Management (CRM) Software: For real estate investors, keeping strong relationships with customers, partners, and fellow investors is important. CRM software allows you to handle leads, track interactions, and nurture relationships successfully. By organizing and centralizing contact information, emails, and notes, you can keep a personalized approach to conversation and provide excellent customer service. CRM tools can also help you stay on top of follow-ups and streamline your marketing efforts, Ensuring you never miss out on possible investment possibilities.

Embracing Smart Home Technology: The rise of the Internet of Things (IoT) has given birth to smart home technology, which has significant effects on real estate owners. Smart home features, such as automated lighting, temperature control, security systems, and smart locks, are not only attractive to tech-savvy renters but also offer useful benefits for property management. These features can be directly controlled and watched, allowing you to easily address maintenance issues, enhance energy economy, and ensure the security of your rental properties. As a result, smart houses can lead to better renter happiness and increased property value.

Real Estate Data Analytics: Data analytics has emerged as a powerful tool for real estate investors looking to gain greater insights into market trends, property values, and business possibilities. With access to extensive data sets and advanced analytics tools, investors can perform robust market research and make data-driven choices. Real estate data analytics can show useful information about market demand, pricing trends, past success, and future Forecasts. Armed with this information, you can spot profitable markets, assess risks, and develop effective business strategies.

Embracing real estate technology is no longer a choice but a necessity for modern owners. As technology continues to change, staying updated on the latest advancements and integrating relevant tools into your investment approach can give you a competitive edge in the dynamic real estate market. Whether you're a seasoned investor or just starting, embracing the power of real estate technology can ease your processes, improve decision-making, and pave the way for long-term success in your investment journey.

Using Data to Make Informed Decisions

In the dynamic world of real estate buying, data has emerged as a game-changer, enabling investors to make well-informed and strategic choices. Gone are the days of depending solely on gut feelings and stories. In this chapter, we'll dig deeper into the power of data and explore how it can help you become a better and more successful real estate investor.

Market Research and Analysis: One of the key ways data can help you is by offering valuable market research and analysis. With the wealth of online tools and platforms, getting real estate info has never been easier. You can gain insights into property prices, past trends, market supply and demand dynamics, and local economic data. By studying market data, you can spot possible growth areas, anticipate market trends, and better understand the general health of a particular location.

Comparable Sales Analysis: Performing a comparison analysis of recent property sales, also known as "comps," is an important step in the business process. This research includes studying similar properties that have recently sold in the target area. By comparing factors such as size, location, state, and sale price, you can gauge the fair market value of a property you're interested in. Comparable sales analysis helps you determine whether a possible investment property is priced fairly or if there's room for negotiation.

Rental Market Analysis: For investors focused on rental properties, having a rental market analysis is important. Data on rental prices, vacancy rates, and Tenant demographics can provide insights into the desire for rental homes in a given area. Understanding the local rental market helps you set competitive rental prices, forecast possible rental income, and make informed choices about property management.

Demographic and Economic Trends: Demographic and economic data play a vital role in evaluating the long-term prospects of an investment site. By studying aspects such as population growth, job trends, median household income, and infrastructure development, you can gain a better knowledge of a market's sustainability. A growing population and a strong job market can signal a healthy and hopeful real estate market.

Real Estate Investment Metrics:
Data-driven buyers depend on various key performance indicators (KPIs) to measure the financial stability of a property. Some important investment indicators include:

Return on Investment (ROI): A measure of the property's profitability, measured by dividing the net profit by the starting investment.

Cash Flow: The difference between rental income and expenses, showing the property's ability to make positive cash flow.

Cap Rate (Capitalization Rate): The ratio of a property's net operating income to its current market value, giving insight into its possible return on investment.

Gross Rent Multiplier (GRM): A quick way to assess a property's income potential by dividing the property price by the gross renting income.

Data-Driven Risk Assessment: Data can also help in risk assessment and reduction. By carefully analyzing market data and property-specific information, you can spot possible risks linked with an investment. These risks may include market volatility, renter turnover rates, possible repair costs, or changes in local laws. Armed with this knowledge, you can develop contingency plans and make calculated choices to protect your possessions.

Embracing Technology for Data Analysis: To successfully grasp the power of data, it's important to leverage technology and analysis tools. Real Estate business tools, spreadsheets, and data visualization platforms can help you organize, analyze, and understand the vast amount of data available. These tools simplify the decision-making process, making it easier for you to spot trends and patterns that may not be immediately apparent.

In conclusion, data is a formidable partner for real estate owners seeking success in a competitive market. By conducting detailed market research, performing comparative analysis, and utilizing technology, you can make informed choices, minimize risks, and position yourself for profitable possibilities. Always remember that data should not be the sole determinant of your investment decisions, but rather a useful resource that complements your experience, instincts, and general investment strategy.

Real Estate Investment Software and Tools

In the fast-evolving world of real estate investing, the power of technology cannot be overstated. Real estate investing apps and tools have become important in streamlining processes, organizing data, and optimizing decision-making for owners of all Experience levels. In this chapter, we'll explore a variety of real estate investment apps and tools that can allow you to take your investment game to the next level.

Property Analysis and Valuation Software: One of the most critical aspects of real estate buying is studying and evaluating possible properties correctly. Real estate investment research software helps you crunch the numbers and analyze the financial viability of an investment. These tools usually take into account factors like property price, rental income, costs, funding terms, and growth potential. By using such tools, you can make well-informed choices based on thorough cash flow analysis, return on investment (ROI) projections, and estimated property values over time.

Market Research and Data Aggregation Platforms: Staying on top of market trends and conditions is important for a successful real estate business. Market research and data aggregation tools compile and analyze vast amounts of data, giving insights into local real estate markets. These tools provide information about past property prices, rental rates, vacancy rates, population growth, economic factors, And other crucial data points. Armed with this information, you can spot areas with growth prospects and make informed decisions about where to invest.

Customer Relationship Management (CRM) Software:
Building and maintaining strong connections with possible buyers, sellers, and partners is important in real estate investing. CRM software is meant to help you organize your contacts, track interactions, and nurture leads successfully. By organizing your contacts and conversation, you can improve your networking efforts, ensure timely follow-ups, and eventually increase the chances of finishing deals.

Property Management Software: For owners with rental homes, property management software is a game-changer. These systems simplify and automate various property management chores, such as rent collection, lease management, maintenance tracking, and tenant screening. Property management tools can help you stay organized, save time, and ensure that your properties are well-maintained, leading to more pleased renters.

Real Estate Crowdfunding Platforms: Real estate crowdfunding has emerged as a new way to invest in real estate projects collectively. These sites allow individual investors to pool their funds and invest in properties or development projects that would usually require significant cash. Crowdfunding sites provide access to a wide range of investment possibilities, from residential properties to industrial projects. This democratization of real estate investing offers freedom, variety, and the possibility for better returns.

Virtual Reality (VR) and Augmented Reality (AR) Tools:
Incorporating VR and AR technology into the real estate investing process can be a game-changer, especially when it comes to property review and marketing. With VR and AR tools, you can virtually tour properties, allowing you to assess their features and potential without physically viewing each place. Additionally, these technologies can improve property marketing efforts by offering full and engaging experiences for potential buyers or renters.

Property Tax Analysis Software: Understanding the tax effects of real estate purchases is important for Improving your profits. Property tax analysis software helps you figure out property taxes, measure possible deductions, and explore tax-saving strategies. By correctly estimating your tax bills, you can better plan your funds and maximize the profitability of your assets.

Online Property Listing and Investment Platforms: Online property listing platforms have changed the way properties are bought and sold. These platforms bring together buyers, sellers, dealers, and investors in a centralized community, making it easier to find business possibilities. Some platforms also offer investment-specific features, such as thorough property information, market data, and user-friendly interfaces that ease the investing process.

Incorporating real estate investing software and tools into your business journey can significantly enhance your efficiency, productivity, and total success. As technology continues to advance, keeping informed of the latest tools and trends can give you a competitive edge in the ever-evolving real estate market. Whether you're a seasoned investor or just starting, accepting these technologies will allow you to make informed choices, capitalize On lucrative chances, and build a successful real estate investment portfolio.

Embracing Smart Home Technology

In the ever-evolving world of real estate, adopting smart home technology has emerged as a game-changer for investors and property owners. As the Internet of Things (IoT) continues to revolutionize various sectors, it has found a natural fit in the real estate sector, giving an array of benefits to both owners and renters alike. In this chapter, we'll dive deeper into the world of smart home technology and explore the numerous benefits it brings to your real estate business strategy.

Enhancing Tenant Experience: In today's competitive rental market, offering a smooth and modern living experience is a key difference for drawing and keeping renters. Smart home technology offers a range of features that can greatly improve the renter experience. From remote-controlled thermostats and automatic lighting systems to voice-activated virtual helpers, renters can enjoy greater comfort and convenience in their daily lives. Smart locks and video doorbells Also provide an added layer of security, creating a sense of safety and peace of mind for residents.

Improving Property Management Efficiency: Investors and property managers can leverage smart home technology to improve various management chores. Property management software integrated with smart devices allows for online tracking and control of property systems. For instance, you can directly change the temperature, track energy usage, and receive real-time alerts for maintenance problems. These capabilities decrease the need for real on-site trips, save time, and allow more efficient resource allocation.

Cost Savings and Energy Efficiency: Smart home technology adds to environmental safety and cost savings by optimizing energy usage. Smart thermostats can learn the residents' tastes and build energy-efficient temperature plans, resulting in reduced utility bills. Motion sensors can turn off lights when rooms are vacant, and smart irrigation systems can change watering plans based on weather conditions, saving water resources. Not only does this help the earth, but it also makes your home more attractive to eco-conscious tenants.

Increased Property Value and Attractiveness: Homes built with cutting-edge smart technology tend to command higher renting rates and sales prices. Smart homes have become linked with modernity and luxury, appealing to tech-savvy renters wanting the latest comforts. Investing in smart home upgrades can raise your property's perceived value and set it apart from rival listings.

Remote Property Monitoring and Security: For real estate owners who own properties in different places, smart home technology offers an important edge in remote property monitoring. Through smart security cams and sensors, you can keep a watchful eye on your property, receive instant tips for suspicious activities, and maintain overall security even from miles away. This level of control instills trust and lowers the risks involved with managing properties from a distance.

Personalized Home Automation: With the freedom of smart home technology, property owners can create automation to meet specific needs. For instance, you can program automated welcome messages for new tenants, plan regular maintenance reminders, or set up virtual tours for potential Renters. Personalization allows you to create a unique and memorable experience for your tenants, promoting good reviews and word-of-mouth recommendations.

Data-Driven Insights for Better Decision Making: The data collected through smart home devices can provide useful insights into tenant behavior and property usage trends. By studying this data, you can find areas for improvement, implement energy-efficient changes, and boost renter happiness. Additionally, these data-driven insights can help you in making data-backed business choices, increasing the potential for higher returns.

As the smart home technology market continues to expand, real estate investors must stay updated about the latest trends and offers. Embracing smart home technology is not only a forward-thinking method but also a practical investment in the future of your real estate business. By combining smart devices and automation solutions, you can create a modern, efficient, and attractive living experience for your renters while optimizing your property management processes for better success.

Chapter 10
Scaling Your Real Estate Portfolio

Congratulations! You've successfully delved into the world of real estate trading and achieved some great results. Now, it's time to take your game to the next level by growing your real estate business. Scaling refers to the process of growing your investments carefully and gradually, with the end goal of increasing your wealth and achieving financial freedom. This chapter will guide you through the key strategies and considerations for scaling your real estate business successfully.

Assessing Your Current Portfolio:
Before starting any scaling efforts, it's important to take a step back and review your current portfolio. Evaluate your present properties, their results, and your general investment plan. Ask yourself the following questions:

Which properties are providing the most important returns?

Are there any failing assets that might need to be sold or improved?

What is the general cash flow and revenue of your portfolio?

Are there any similar themes or patterns in your good investments that you can replicate?

Understanding your current portfolio's strengths and weaknesses will help you make informed choices and set clear goals for scaling.

Defining Your Scaling Goals:

Clearly describing your growth goals is crucial for setting your path forward. Consider the following factors when setting your objectives:

Financial Targets: Determine how much wealth you want to collect through your real estate ventures. Set clear financial goals for each stage of scaling.

Portfolio Size: Decide on the number of buildings you aim to own or the total value of your portfolio.

Timeframe: Establish a realistic timeline for meeting your growth goals. Scaling takes time and careful planning, so be patient but determined.

Financing and Capital Sources:
One of the main challenges in scaling your business is getting the necessary funding. As you aim to buy more properties, you'll likely need additional cash. Consider the following options:

Leverage Existing Equity: If your current properties have increased in value, you may be able to use their equity as a down payment for new purchases.

Partnering with Investors: Seek out like-minded investors who can co-invest in properties with you, sharing both the financial load and possible profits.

Creative Financing: Explore creative financing choices such as seller financing, private loans, or crowdfunding sites.

Geographic Diversification:
Expanding your real estate portfolio doesn't generally mean getting multiple homes in the same area. Consider diversifying regionally to lower risk

and take advantage of different market situations. Conduct a thorough study on possible markets, considering things like job growth, population trends, and economic security.

Property Types and Asset Classes:
Scaling your business may involve diversifying the types of buildings you invest in. You could study different asset types, such as residential, business, industrial, or mixed-use properties. Each asset class comes with its unique advantages and challenges, so ensure you understand the specific nuances of each before making financial choices.

Professional Support and Team Building:
As your business grows, handling everything on your own might become overwhelming. Consider building a reliable team of professionals, including property managers, real estate salespeople, contractors, and lawyers. A strong support system will help you improve operations and free up your time to focus on strategic decisions.

Risk Management and Exit Strategies:
Scaling involves taking calculated risks, but it's important to have strong risk management strategies

in place. Evaluate possible risks connected with each investment and build backup plans to avoid them. Additionally, outline clear exit strategies for properties that may not perform as expected, Ensuring you can divest if necessary without suffering significant losses.

Continual Learning and Adaptation:
The real estate market is active and constantly changing. To successfully grow your portfolio, commit to ongoing education and keeping up-to-date with industry trends. Be open to adapting your strategies based on market shifts, changing laws, and new possibilities.

Scaling your real estate business takes drive, patience, and a well-thought-out plan. By setting clear goals, diversifying strategically, and assembling a reliable team, you can slowly grow your wealth and achieve long-term financial success through real estate investment. Remember that scaling is a process, so enjoy each milestone and continue learning along the way. Happy growing!

Strategies for Portfolio Growth

Congratulations! You've successfully started your journey into real estate investing and built a strong base with your initial homes. Now it's time to explore the exciting world of capital growth. In this Chapter, we'll delve deeper into various strategies that can help you grow your real estate holdings and take your investment trip to new heights. Remember, growth takes careful planning, calculated risk-taking, and a commitment to constant learning. Let's review some key methods for growing your real estate portfolio.

Diversification:
One important concept of portfolio growth is diversity. As you look to grow, consider diversifying your investments across different types of buildings, regions, and asset classes. This strategy can help reduce risk and protect your portfolio against changes in individual markets. For instance, if you started with residential buildings, consider spreading out into business, industrial, or mixed-use areas. Each area has its unique advantages and challenges, and diversification allows you to capitalize on a range of possibilities.

Value-Add Opportunities:

Seeking out value-add possibilities is another powerful approach for wealth growth. These are homes with untapped potential or in need of renovation and growth. By buying such properties at A lower cost and making strategic improvements, you can increase their worth greatly. Value-add homes can provide a higher return on investment (ROI) compared to turnkey properties, making them attractive adds to your portfolio.

Joint Ventures and Partnerships:
As your goals grow, you might find it difficult to pay for larger acquisitions on your own. Joint ventures and partnerships can be excellent ways for growing your portfolio without overextending yourself financially. Collaborating with other experienced owners or real estate workers can bring additional resources, knowledge, and access to a bigger network of possibilities.

Leveraging Equity and Cash-Out Refinancing:
If you've built equity in your current properties, consider tapping that equity to fund new assets. Cash-out refinancing allows you to access the wealth in your properties by refinancing your current mortgage and getting the difference in cash.

This approach allows you to use the proceeds to buy additional properties or make improvements to your current ones.

1031 Exchange:
The 1031 exchange is a strong tax-deferral technique that can fuel portfolio growth. This clause in the U.S. tax code allows you to delay capital gains taxes on the sale of an investment property if you reinvest the profits into a "like-kind" property within specific time frames. Utilizing the 1031 swap allows you to compound your gains by deferring taxes and reinvesting the full amount into new homes.

Real Estate Crowdfunding:
In recent years, real estate crowdfunding has appeared as an accessible and flexible way to invest in different projects with relatively low cash needs. Crowdfunding platforms pool funds from multiple investors to support real estate projects. Participating in real estate crowdfunding allows you to spread your investments across multiple buildings and places without the need for hands-on management.

Market Research and Emerging Trends:

Stay vigilant about market trends and emerging possibilities in the real estate field. A thorough study can show new or untapped markets that offer great promise for growth. Keep an eye on demographic Changes, economic indicators, and government policies that may affect the real estate market. Being informed about market dynamics will position you to make well-informed choices and capitalize on new trends.

Reinvestment and Compounding:
As you create rental income and profit from your investments, consider reinvesting a part of these earnings back into your portfolio. The power of compounding can work wonders over time, allowing your stock to grow greatly. Reinvesting profits can help you buy more properties or fund value-add projects, accelerating your portfolio's growth.

Long-Term Vision and Patience:
Portfolio growth is a journey that needs a long-term strategy and patience. It's important to set reasonable goals and keep a steady, sustainable pace. Avoid the urge to rush into investments without careful thought. Sometimes, the best chances come to those

who wait and analyze each possible investment with prudence.

Continuous Learning and Adaptation:
The real estate market is active and ever-changing. To successfully grow your business, commit to constant learning and adaptation. Stay updated on business trends, attend classes, workshops, and conferences, and network with other investors. Learning from experienced professionals and changing your strategies as needed will allow you to handle the market's changes and grab opportunities as they arise.

In conclusion, portfolio growth in real estate is an exciting and fulfilling undertaking. By diversifying your interests, finding value-add opportunities, making smart relationships, and staying informed, you can chart a successful path toward building a robust and thriving real estate portfolio. Remember that each investor's journey is unique, so find the methods that match your goals and risk tolerance. With commitment and a well-executed plan, you'll be on your way to achieving real estate riches!

Balancing Diversification and Concentration

Congratulations! By this point in your real estate investment journey, you've likely bought one or more properties and are feeling the excitement of being a real estate owner. As you continue on this road, you'll meet a crucial aspect of successful investing: finding the right balance between diversification and focus.

Diversification is the practice of spreading your investments across different types of real estate assets, regions, and markets. It's often praised as a risk-reduction approach. By diversifying your portfolio, you can reduce the effect of any single property's bad performance or market downturns. On the other hand, concentration means focusing your capital on a specific type of property, a particular area, or a niche market. Concentration can lead to higher returns when you find beneficial opportunities, but it also carries a higher risk if the market faces challenges.

Both diversification and concentration have their benefits, so it's important to strike a mix that aligns with your financial goals, risk tolerance, and Long-term vision. Here are some key considerations to help you make informed decisions:

Defining Your Investment Objectives: Start by revisiting your financial goals. Are you seeking steady cash flow or looking for big appreciation? Your goals will influence how you divide your resources between diversified assets and concentrated stocks.

Understanding Risk and Reward: Diversification can act as a safety net during economic downturns, while focus can increase your gains during market upswings. Evaluate your readiness to accept danger and your capacity to handle possible losses.

Researching Real Estate Markets: Perform in-depth research on different real estate markets and submarkets. Identify areas with good growth potential, favorable demographics, and economic security. Consider diversifying across areas to gain from different economic forces.

Assessing Asset Classes: Real estate includes a wide range of asset classes, such as residential, business, industrial, and retail buildings. Each class has its Risk-reward ratio. A diverse portfolio may include a mix of these asset types to balance your risk exposure.

Analyzing Cash Flow vs. Appreciation Potential: Some homes create steady rental income, giving constant cash flow, while others hold greater potential for long-term appreciation. Strike a mix between cash flow-generating properties and those with appreciation potential to secure both short-term security and long-term growth.

Considering Risk Segmentation: Diversification can stretch beyond property kinds and places. Consider segmenting your assets based on the risky nature of buildings. High-risk properties may offer higher returns, but they should be balanced with lower-risk, safe investments.

Leveraging Professional Advice: Seek advice from experienced real estate professionals, such as financial advisors, real estate salespeople, and property managers. They can give insights into market trends, possible investment possibilities, and the general health of specific regions.

Evaluating Economic Indicators: Keep a close eye on economic indicators that could affect your investments, such as interest rates, job data, population growth, and building developments. These indicators can guide your diversification and concentration tactics.

Monitoring Portfolio Performance: Regularly review the performance of your investments to measure whether your diversification and concentration tactics are matched with your goals. Adjust your method as needed based on market conditions and your changing financial situation.

Embracing Flexibility: Real estate markets are active and can change quickly. Be prepared to adapt your plan as situations evolve. Being flexible helps you to capitalize on emerging chances and handle challenges effectively.

Remember, the right mix between diversification and concentration is unique to each trader.

Continuously teach yourself about real estate markets, stay updated on industry trends, and stay true to your long-term vision. By doing so, you can Build a sturdy and profitable real estate business that stands the test of time. Happy buying!

Long-Term Wealth Building and Exit Strategies

Congratulations! By this point in the book, you've learned about the ins and outs of investing in real estate, and now it's time to dig into the crucial aspect of long-term wealth-building and exit plans. This chapter will equip you with the information to maximize your real estate purchases, protect your financial future, and achieve your desired level of prosperity.

Building a Strong Foundation:
Before getting into exit strategies, it's important to stress the importance of building a strong base for your real estate business. This means continually working on getting high-quality properties, managing them well, and keeping up with market trends. Strong roots will ensure that your investment homes stay desirable to potential renters or buyers, which is important for long-term success.

The Power of Equity:

As you hold onto your investment properties, they will likely increase over time, thanks to both market trends and property changes. The growth in property value leads to the collection of equity, which is one of the most powerful wealth-building tools in real estate. Understanding how to maximize this wealth can significantly impact your financial success.

Refinancing for Growth:

Refinancing is a technique that allows you to tap into the equity of your properties to fund the acquisition of additional business opportunities. By refinancing, you can access funds without selling your properties, allowing you to expand your portfolio and improve your potential for long-term wealth growth. However, it's important to approach refinancing thoughtfully and consider the impact on your cash flow and general investment strategy.

1031 Exchange:

The 1031 exchange is a strong tool that allows real estate owners to defer capital gains taxes when selling one investment property and getting another like-kind property within a specific timeframe. This approach enables the preservation of capital and allows you to reinvest your gains into more Substantial and possibly more profitable properties. Utilizing a 1031 swap can boost your portfolio's growth while minimizing tax liabilities.

Rental Income and Passive Cash Flow:
Investing in rental homes can be an excellent source of idle income. Rental income provides a steady stream of cash flow that can be reinvested to buy additional properties or cover your costs, thereby increasing your total financial stability and wealth-building potential. Properly managing rental homes and keeping a strong relationship with your renters are important to ensure steady cash flow.

Diversification:
As you grow on your real estate business journey, diversification becomes increasingly important. Consider expanding your portfolio to include different property types, regions, and investing methods. Diversification can reduce risks connected with market fluctuations and economic downturns, protecting your wealth in the long run.

Timing the Market vs. Time in the Market:

Timing the real estate market correctly is incredibly difficult, if not impossible. Instead of trying to Predict market highs and lows, focus on the power of time in the market. Long-term investing helps you to ride out market fluctuations and gain from general growth. Patience and a buy-and-hold method are often key factors in building substantial wealth in real estate.

Knowing When to Sell:
While long-term buying is a proven wealth-building plan, there may come a time when selling an investment property makes sense. Identifying the right time to sell takes a thorough study of various factors, such as market conditions, your financial goals, and your total portfolio success. Properly timing your exit can help you capitalize on gains and reinvest in possibly more lucrative opportunities.

Legacy and Estate Planning:
As your real estate business grows, it's important to consider your legacy and estate planning. Developing a clear plan for the future distribution of your assets can help ensure that your hard-earned wealth benefits your loved ones and chosen recipients in the most tax-efficient way.

In conclusion, this chapter shows the value of long-term wealth-building and exit plans in real estate investing. By keeping a strong base, leveraging equity, applying intelligent refinancing, and diversifying your assets, you can place yourself for lasting financial success. Embrace the power of time in the market, seriously consider when to sell, and engage in careful estate planning to protect your financial inheritance for generations to come. Happy buying!

Conclusion

In "Real Estate Riches: A Comprehensive Guide to Successful Investing," we have dug into the world of real estate investment with a focus on enabling you to make informed choices and achieve financial wealth. Throughout this book, we have studied various parts of the real estate market, giving useful insights and practical strategies to help you manage the difficulties of this lucrative field.

Understanding the intricacies of the real estate market is important, and we have given you a thorough review of supply and demand, market trends, and how to find potential places. Armed with this information, you can place yourself to take chances and stay ahead of market trends.

Having clear financial goals and a well-defined plan is important for success. We have covered different investment methods and risk assessment techniques, allowing you to tailor your plan to match your financial goals and risk tolerance.

Financing your real estate projects is often a critical step, and we have explored a range of financing Options, from traditional mortgages to creative funding solutions, enabling you to secure the necessary capital to continue your interests securely.

Finding profitable investment homes requires careful study and analysis. By utilizing effective property search methods and analyzing potential returns, you will be able to find properties with strong financial potential.

Conducting due research is important to protecting your assets. We have covered the important aspects of property value, legal issues, and ownership proof to ensure you make informed choices and reduce possible risks.

Negotiation skills play a vital part in real estate deals, and we have provided methods to help you handle talks successfully, achieving win-win results with sellers, agents, and buyers.

Understanding the tax effects of your real estate purchases is important for making profits. We have studied different tax tactics, deductions, and tax-efficient holding structures to help you improve your financial returns.

Property care and repair are essential to long-term success as a real estate owner. By choosing reliable property managers, conducting thorough renter screenings, and following care best practices, you can protect your investment and create positive cash flow.

Incorporating technology and data analytics into your real estate projects can provide a competitive edge. We have stressed the value of deploying real estate technology and data to make data-driven choices that can improve your business results.

As your real estate business grows, we have covered methods for growing and handling your investments. Balancing diversification and concentration while keeping a focus on long-term wealth-building and exit plans will allow you to achieve continuous success in real estate.

In conclusion, "Real Estate Riches: A Comprehensive Guide to Successful Investing" gives you the information, tools, and methods needed to succeed in the world of real estate investment. Whether you're a seasoned investor looking to grow your portfolio or a beginner Entering into this exciting field, this book offers useful insights that can lead to financial happiness. Remember that success in the real estate business requires constant learning, flexibility, and a desire to take measured chances. Armed with the information given in this book, you are now ready to start on a satisfying journey to build permanent wealth through smart and planned real estate investment.

www.ingramcontent.com/pod-product-compliance
Lightning Source LLC
Chambersburg PA
CBHW070847260726
48661CB00004B/1286